My *Memory Pal* Journal

A Record of My Daily Life So I'll Remember What the Heck Happened

ISBN: 9781795448123

Rebecca Livermore
Professional Content Creation
Littleton, CO

Dedication

This book is dedicated to my dear friend, Sherry Johnson, and all the fond memories we share.

How to Use this Journal

This journal was designed to be used in a way that works best for YOU. I recommend that you choose which things you most want to remember, and be as consistent as possible in writing those things down.

Forming the Journaling Habit

The best way to form the journaling habit is to tie it to other things. For instance, you may say, "As soon as I eat, I record what I ate in my journal." In that case, the act of eating is a trigger to journal. You can also set up phone reminders to go off throughout the day to remind you to write things down.

Since the goal is to record as much as possible so you'll remember what happened, make it a practice to keep your journal and a pen or pencil nearby or where you'll see it frequently.

It's Okay to Leave Blanks!

By the way, if something doesn't apply to you personally, leave it blank! For example, while there is room to record medication you take three times a day, you may only take medication once or twice a day or perhaps not at all. You can leave those parts of your journal blank, or use the space to write down things specific to your life.

Today I Talked To...

Use the "Today I talked to" section to record conversations of every type. This includes everything from phone conversations, to chats with neighbors, to in-person conversations with friends, family, and doctors. Simply jot down a sentence or two about what you talked about immediately after (or even during!) the conversation.

What Concerned or Frightened You

Use this section to record any type of concern or fear. For instance, if you have a medical test or procedure that worries you, or got an upsetting phone call, or a big bill in the mail, jot it down. Share those concerns with a trusted friend or family member.

What You're Grateful For

Expressing gratitude is one of the best ways to see the world in a more positive light. Make it a habit to write down one thing you're grateful for each day. By the way, it's totally fine to write down the same thing more than once!

Other Thoughts or Experiences You Want to Remember

The "Other thoughts or experiences I want to remember" is a place to jot down anything not covered in the other aspects of the journal. Consider these examples:

- What made you smile today?
- What made you say, "wow!" today?
- Did you run any errands today?
- Did you spend any money today?
- Is there anything you need to discuss with your doctor?
- And of course, anything else you want to write about!

Turn the page to begin your journaling adventure!

☐ Su   ☐ Mo   ☐ Tu   ☐ We   ☐ Th   ☐ Fr   ☐ Sa

Date _____

How I feel today (physically): _____

How I feel today (emotionally): _____

Medication I Took

Morning _____

_____

Afternoon _____

_____

Evening _____

_____

What I Ate

Morning _____

_____

Afternoon _____

_____

Evening _____

_____

Glasses of Water

Today I talked to:

_____ About _____

_____

_____ About _____

_____

_____ About _____

_____

_____About _____

_____

Things that frightened or concerned me today:

_____

_____

Today I am grateful for:

_____

_____

Other thoughts or experiences I want to remember:

_____

_____

_____

_____

_____

☐ Su ☐ Mo ☐ Tu ☐ We ☐ Th ☐ Fr ☐ Sa

Date _____

How I feel today (physically): _____

How I feel today (emotionally): _____

Medication I Took

Morning _____

_____

Afternoon _____

_____

Evening _____

_____

What I Ate

Morning _____

_____

Afternoon _____

_____

Evening _____

_____

Glasses of Water

Today I talked to:

_____ About _____

_____

_____ About _____

_____

_____ About _____

_____

_____About _____

_____

Things that frightened or concerned me today:

_____

_____

Today I am grateful for:

_____

_____

Other thoughts or experiences I want to remember:

_____

_____

_____

_____

_____

☐ Su   ☐ Mo   ☐ Tu   ☐ We   ☐ Th   ☐ Fr   ☐ Sa

Date _____

How I feel today (physically): _____

How I feel today (emotionally): _____

Medication I Took

Morning _____

_____

Afternoon _____

_____

Evening _____

_____

What I Ate

Morning _____

_____

Afternoon _____

_____

Evening _____

_____

Glasses of Water

Today I talked to:

_____ About _____

_____

_____ About _____

_____

_____ About _____

_____

_____ About _____

_____

Things that frightened or concerned me today:

_____

_____

Today I am grateful for:

_____

_____

Other thoughts or experiences I want to remember:

_____

_____

_____

_____

_____

☐ Su   ☐ Mo   ☐ Tu   ☐ We   ☐ Th   ☐ Fr   ☐ Sa

Date _____

How I feel today (physically): _____

How I feel today (emotionally): _____

Medication I Took

Morning _____

_____

Afternoon _____

_____

Evening _____

_____

What I Ate

Morning _____

_____

Afternoon _____

_____

Evening _____

_____

Glasses of Water

☐   ☐   ☐   ☐

☐   ☐   ☐   ☐

Today I talked to:

_____ About _____

_____

_____ About _____

_____

_____ About _____

_____

_____ About _____

_____

Things that frightened or concerned me today:

_____

_____

Today I am grateful for:

_____

_____

Other thoughts or experiences I want to remember:

_____

_____

_____

_____

_____

☐ Su ☐ Mo ☐ Tu ☐ We ☐ Th ☐ Fr ☐ Sa

Date _____

How I feel today (physically): _____

How I feel today (emotionally): _____

Medication I Took

Morning _____

_____

Afternoon _____

_____

Evening _____

_____

What I Ate

Morning _____

_____

Afternoon _____

_____

Evening _____

_____

Glasses of Water

Today I talked to:

_____ About _____

_____

_____ About _____

_____

_____ About _____

_____

_____About _____

_____

Things that frightened or concerned me today:

_____

_____

Today I am grateful for:

_____

_____

Other thoughts or experiences I want to remember:

_____

_____

_____

_____

_____

☐ Su ☐ Mo ☐ Tu ☐ We ☐ Th ☐ Fr ☐ Sa

Date _____

How I feel today (physically): _____

How I feel today (emotionally): _____

Medication I Took

Morning _____

_____

Afternoon _____

_____

Evening _____

_____

What I Ate

Morning _____

_____

Afternoon _____

_____

Evening _____

_____

Glasses of Water

Today I talked to:

_____ About _____

_____

_____ About _____

_____

_____ About _____

_____

_____ About _____

_____

Things that frightened or concerned me today:

_____

_____

Today I am grateful for:

_____

_____

Other thoughts or experiences I want to remember:

_____

_____

_____

_____

_____

☐ Su ☐ Mo ☐ Tu ☐ We ☐ Th ☐ Fr ☐ Sa

Date _____

How I feel today (physically): _____

How I feel today (emotionally): _____

Medication I Took

Morning _____

_____

Afternoon _____

_____

Evening _____

_____

What I Ate

Morning _____

_____

Afternoon _____

_____

Evening _____

_____

Glasses of Water

Today I talked to:

_____ About _____

_____

_____ About _____

_____

_____ About _____

_____

_____ About _____

_____

Things that frightened or concerned me today:

_____

_____

Today I am grateful for:

_____

_____

Other thoughts or experiences I want to remember:

_____

_____

_____

_____

_____

☐Su   ☐Mo   ☐Tu   ☐We   ☐Th   ☐Fr   ☐Sa

Date   _____

How I feel today (physically): _____

How I feel today (emotionally): _____

Medication I Took

Morning _____

_____

Afternoon _____

_____

Evening _____

_____

What I Ate

Morning _____

_____

Afternoon _____

_____

Evening _____

_____

Glasses of Water

Today I talked to:

_____ About _____

_____

_____ About _____

_____

_____ About _____

_____

_____ About _____

_____

Things that frightened or concerned me today:

_____

_____

Today I am grateful for:

_____

_____

Other thoughts or experiences I want to remember:

_____

_____

_____

_____

_____

☐Su ☐Mo ☐Tu ☐We ☐Th ☐Fr ☐Sa

Date _____

How I feel today (physically): _____

How I feel today (emotionally): _____

Medication I Took

Morning _____

_____

Afternoon _____

_____

Evening _____

_____

What I Ate

Morning _____

_____

Afternoon _____

_____

Evening _____

_____

Glasses of Water

Today I talked to:

_____ About _____

_____ About _____

_____ About _____

_____ About _____

Things that frightened or concerned me today:

_____

_____

Today I am grateful for:

_____

_____

Other thoughts or experiences I want to remember:

_____

_____

_____

_____

_____

☐Su   ☐Mo   ☐Tu   ☐We   ☐Th   ☐Fr   ☐Sa

Date _____

How I feel today (physically): _____

How I feel today (emotionally): _____

Medication I Took

Morning _____

_____

Afternoon _____

_____

Evening _____

_____

What I Ate

Morning _____

_____

Afternoon _____

_____

Evening _____

_____

Glasses of Water

Today I talked to:

_____ About _____

_____

_____ About _____

_____

_____ About _____

_____

_____ About _____

_____

Things that frightened or concerned me today:

_____

_____

Today I am grateful for:

_____

_____

Other thoughts or experiences I want to remember:

_____

_____

_____

_____

_____

☐ Su   ☐ Mo   ☐ Tu   ☐ We   ☐ Th   ☐ Fr   ☐ Sa

Date _____

How I feel today (physically): _____

How I feel today (emotionally): _____

Medication I Took

Morning _____

_____

Afternoon _____

_____

Evening _____

_____

What I Ate

Morning _____

_____

Afternoon _____

_____

Evening _____

_____

Glasses of Water

Today I talked to:

_____ About _____

_____ About _____

_____ About _____

_____ About _____

Things that frightened or concerned me today:

_____

_____

Today I am grateful for:

_____

_____

Other thoughts or experiences I want to remember:

_____

_____

_____

_____

_____

☐ Su　　☐ Mo　　☐ Tu　　☐ We　　☐ Th　　☐ Fr　　☐ Sa

Date　　_____

How I feel today (physically): _____

How I feel today (emotionally): _____

Medication I Took

Morning　_____

_____

Afternoon　_____

_____

Evening　　_____

_____

What I Ate

Morning　_____

_____

Afternoon　_____

_____

Evening　_____

_____

Glasses of Water

☐　　☐　　☐　　☐

☐　　☐　　☐　　☐

Today I talked to:

_____ About _____

_____

_____ About _____

_____

_____ About _____

_____

_____ About _____

_____

Things that frightened or concerned me today:

_____

_____

Today I am grateful for:

_____

_____

Other thoughts or experiences I want to remember:

_____

_____

_____

_____

_____

☐Su　　☐Mo　　☐Tu　　☐We　　☐Th　　☐Fr　　☐Sa

Date　_____

How I feel today (physically): _____

How I feel today (emotionally): _____

Medication I Took

Morning _____

_____

Afternoon _____

_____

Evening _____

_____

What I Ate

Morning _____

_____

Afternoon _____

_____

Evening _____

_____

Glasses of Water

Today I talked to:

_____ About _____

_____ About _____

_____ About _____

_____ About _____

Things that frightened or concerned me today:

_____

_____

Today I am grateful for:

_____

_____

Other thoughts or experiences I want to remember:

_____

_____

_____

_____

_____

☐Su ☐Mo ☐Tu ☐We ☐Th ☐Fr ☐Sa

Date _____

How I feel today (physically): _____

How I feel today (emotionally): _____

Medication I Took

Morning _____

_____

Afternoon _____

_____

Evening _____

_____

What I Ate

Morning _____

_____

Afternoon _____

_____

Evening _____

_____

Glasses of Water

Today I talked to:

_____ About _____

_____

_____ About _____

_____

_____ About _____

_____

_____ About _____

_____

Things that frightened or concerned me today:

_____

_____

Today I am grateful for:

_____

_____

Other thoughts or experiences I want to remember:

_____

_____

_____

_____

_____

☐Su ☐Mo ☐Tu ☐We ☐Th ☐Fr ☐Sa

Date _____

How I feel today (physically): _____

How I feel today (emotionally): _____

Medication I Took

Morning _____

_____

Afternoon _____

_____

Evening _____

_____

What I Ate

Morning _____

_____

Afternoon _____

_____

Evening _____

_____

Glasses of Water

Today I talked to:

_____ About _____

_____

_____ About _____

_____

_____ About _____

_____

_____About _____

_____

Things that frightened or concerned me today:

_____

_____

Today I am grateful for:

_____

_____

Other thoughts or experiences I want to remember:

_____

_____

_____

_____

_____

☐Su ☐Mo ☐Tu ☐We ☐Th ☐Fr ☐Sa

Date _____

How I feel today (physically): _____

How I feel today (emotionally): _____

Medication I Took

Morning _____

_____

Afternoon _____

_____

Evening _____

_____

What I Ate

Morning _____

_____

Afternoon _____

_____

Evening _____

_____

Glasses of Water

Today I talked to:

_____ About _____

_____

_____ About _____

_____

_____ About _____

_____

_____ About _____

_____

Things that frightened or concerned me today:

_____

_____

Today I am grateful for:

_____

_____

Other thoughts or experiences I want to remember:

_____

_____

_____

_____

_____

☐ Su ☐ Mo ☐ Tu ☐ We ☐ Th ☐ Fr ☐ Sa

Date _____

How I feel today (physically): _____

How I feel today (emotionally): _____

Medication I Took

Morning _____
_____

Afternoon _____
_____

Evening _____
_____

What I Ate

Morning _____
_____

Afternoon _____
_____

Evening _____
_____

Glasses of Water

Today I talked to:

_____ About _____

_____

_____ About _____

_____

_____ About _____

_____

_____ About _____

_____

Things that frightened or concerned me today:

_____

_____

Today I am grateful for:

_____

_____

Other thoughts or experiences I want to remember:

_____

_____

_____

_____

_____

☐ Su ☐ Mo ☐ Tu ☐ We ☐ Th ☐ Fr ☐ Sa

Date _____

How I feel today (physically): _____

How I feel today (emotionally): _____

Medication I Took

Morning _____

_____

Afternoon _____

_____

Evening _____

_____

What I Ate

Morning _____

_____

Afternoon _____

_____

Evening _____

_____

Glasses of Water

Today I talked to:

_____ About _____

_____

_____ About _____

_____

_____ About _____

_____

_____ About _____

_____

Things that frightened or concerned me today:

_____

_____

Today I am grateful for:

_____

_____

Other thoughts or experiences I want to remember:

_____

_____

_____

_____

_____

☐Su ☐Mo ☐Tu ☐We ☐Th ☐Fr ☐Sa

Date _____

How I feel today (physically): _____

How I feel today (emotionally): _____

Medication I Took

Morning _____

_____

Afternoon _____

_____

Evening _____

_____

What I Ate

Morning _____

_____

Afternoon _____

_____

Evening _____

_____

Glasses of Water

Today I talked to:

_____ About _____

_____

_____ About _____

_____

_____ About _____

_____

_____ About _____

_____

Things that frightened or concerned me today:

_____

_____

Today I am grateful for:

_____

_____

Other thoughts or experiences I want to remember:

_____

_____

_____

_____

_____

☐Su   ☐Mo   ☐Tu   ☐We   ☐Th   ☐Fr   ☐Sa

Date _____

How I feel today (physically): _____

How I feel today (emotionally): _____

Medication I Took

Morning _____

_____

Afternoon _____

_____

Evening _____

_____

What I Ate

Morning _____

_____

Afternoon _____

_____

Evening _____

_____

Glasses of Water

Today I talked to:

_____ About _____

_____

_____ About _____

_____

_____ About _____

_____

_____ About _____

_____

Things that frightened or concerned me today:

_____

_____

Today I am grateful for:

_____

_____

Other thoughts or experiences I want to remember:

_____

_____

_____

_____

_____

☐Su ☐Mo ☐Tu ☐We ☐Th ☐Fr ☐Sa

Date _____

How I feel today (physically): _____

How I feel today (emotionally): _____

Medication I Took

Morning _____

_____

Afternoon _____

_____

Evening _____

_____

What I Ate

Morning _____

_____

Afternoon _____

_____

Evening _____

_____

Glasses of Water

Today I talked to:

_____ About _____

_____

_____ About _____

_____

_____ About _____

_____

_____ About _____

_____

Things that frightened or concerned me today:

_____

_____

Today I am grateful for:

_____

_____

Other thoughts or experiences I want to remember:

_____

_____

_____

_____

_____

☐ Su   ☐ Mo   ☐ Tu   ☐ We   ☐ Th   ☐ Fr   ☐ Sa

Date _____

How I feel today (physically): _____

How I feel today (emotionally): _____

Medication I Took

Morning _____

_____

Afternoon _____

_____

Evening _____

_____

What I Ate

Morning _____

_____

Afternoon _____

_____

Evening _____

_____

Glasses of Water

Today I talked to:

_____ About _____

_____

_____ About _____

_____

_____ About _____

_____

_____ About _____

_____

Things that frightened or concerned me today:

_____

_____

Today I am grateful for:

_____

_____

Other thoughts or experiences I want to remember:

_____

_____

_____

_____

☐Su　　☐Mo　　☐Tu　　☐We　　☐Th　　☐Fr　　☐Sa

Date _____

How I feel today (physically): _____

How I feel today (emotionally): _____

Medication I Took

Morning _____

_____

Afternoon _____

_____

Evening _____

_____

What I Ate

Morning _____

_____

Afternoon _____

_____

Evening _____

_____

Glasses of Water

☐　　☐　　☐　　☐

☐　　☐　　☐　　☐

Today I talked to:

_____ About _____

_____

_____ About _____

_____

_____ About _____

_____

_____ About _____

_____

Things that frightened or concerned me today:

_____

_____

Today I am grateful for:

_____

_____

Other thoughts or experiences I want to remember:

_____

_____

_____

_____

_____

☐Su   ☐Mo   ☐Tu   ☐We   ☐Th   ☐Fr   ☐Sa

Date _____

How I feel today (physically): _____

How I feel today (emotionally): _____

Medication I Took

Morning _____

_____

Afternoon _____

_____

Evening _____

_____

What I Ate

Morning _____

_____

Afternoon _____

_____

Evening _____

_____

Glasses of Water

Today I talked to:

_____ About _____

_____

_____ About _____

_____

_____ About _____

_____

_____About _____

_____

Things that frightened or concerned me today:

_____

_____

Today I am grateful for:

_____

_____

Other thoughts or experiences I want to remember:

_____

_____

_____

_____

_____

☐Su   ☐Mo   ☐Tu   ☐We   ☐Th   ☐Fr   ☐Sa

Date _____

How I feel today (physically): _____

How I feel today (emotionally): _____

Medication I Took

Morning _____

_____

Afternoon _____

_____

Evening _____

_____

What I Ate

Morning _____

_____

Afternoon _____

_____

Evening _____

_____

Glasses of Water

Today I talked to:

_____ About _____

_____

_____ About _____

_____

_____ About _____

_____

_____About _____

_____

Things that frightened or concerned me today:

_____

_____

Today I am grateful for:

_____

_____

Other thoughts or experiences I want to remember:

_____

_____

_____

_____

_____

☐Su   ☐Mo   ☐Tu   ☐We   ☐Th   ☐Fr   ☐Sa

Date _____

How I feel today (physically): _____

How I feel today (emotionally): _____

Medication I Took

Morning _____

_____

Afternoon _____

_____

Evening _____

_____

What I Ate

Morning _____

_____

Afternoon _____

_____

Evening _____

_____

Glasses of Water

Today I talked to:

_____ About _____

_____

_____ About _____

_____

_____ About _____

_____

_____ About _____

_____

Things that frightened or concerned me today:

_____

_____

Today I am grateful for:

_____

_____

Other thoughts or experiences I want to remember:

_____

_____

_____

_____

_____

☐Su　　☐Mo　　☐Tu　　☐We　　☐Th　　☐Fr　　☐Sa

Date _____

How I feel today (physically): _____

How I feel today (emotionally): _____

Medication I Took

Morning _____

_____

Afternoon _____

_____

Evening _____

_____

What I Ate

Morning _____

_____

Afternoon _____

_____

Evening _____

_____

Glasses of Water

Today I talked to:

_____ About _____

_____

_____ About _____

_____

_____ About _____

_____

_____ About _____

_____

Things that frightened or concerned me today:

_____

_____

Today I am grateful for:

_____

_____

Other thoughts or experiences I want to remember:

_____

_____

_____

_____

☐ Su ☐ Mo ☐ Tu ☐ We ☐ Th ☐ Fr ☐ Sa

Date _____

How I feel today (physically): _____

How I feel today (emotionally): _____

Medication I Took

Morning _____

_____

Afternoon _____

_____

Evening _____

_____

What I Ate

Morning _____

_____

Afternoon _____

_____

Evening _____

_____

Glasses of Water

☐ ☐ ☐ ☐

☐ ☐ ☐ ☐

Today I talked to:

_____ About _____

_____ About _____

_____ About _____

_____ About _____

Things that frightened or concerned me today:

_____

_____

Today I am grateful for:

_____

_____

Other thoughts or experiences I want to remember:

_____

_____

_____

_____

_____

☐ Su   ☐ Mo   ☐ Tu   ☐ We   ☐ Th   ☐ Fr   ☐ Sa

Date _____

How I feel today (physically): _____

How I feel today (emotionally): _____

Medication I Took

Morning _____

_____

Afternoon _____

_____

Evening _____

_____

What I Ate

Morning _____

_____

Afternoon _____

_____

Evening _____

_____

Glasses of Water

Today I talked to:

_____ About _____

_____

_____ About _____

_____

_____ About _____

_____

_____About _____

_____

Things that frightened or concerned me today:

_____

_____

Today I am grateful for:

_____

_____

Other thoughts or experiences I want to remember:

_____

_____

_____

_____

_____

☐ Su ☐ Mo ☐ Tu ☐ We ☐ Th ☐ Fr ☐ Sa

Date _____

How I feel today (physically): _____

How I feel today (emotionally): _____

Medication I Took

Morning _____

_____

Afternoon _____

_____

Evening _____

_____

What I Ate

Morning _____

_____

Afternoon _____

_____

Evening _____

_____

Glasses of Water

Today I talked to:

_____ About _____

_____

_____ About _____

_____

_____ About _____

_____

_____ About _____

_____

Things that frightened or concerned me today:

_____

_____

Today I am grateful for:

_____

_____

Other thoughts or experiences I want to remember:

_____

_____

_____

_____

_____

☐Su ☐Mo ☐Tu ☐We ☐Th ☐Fr ☐Sa

Date _____

How I feel today (physically): _____

How I feel today (emotionally): _____

Medication I Took

Morning _____

_____

Afternoon _____

_____

Evening _____

_____

What I Ate

Morning _____

_____

Afternoon _____

_____

Evening _____

_____

Glasses of Water

Today I talked to:

_____ About _____

_____

_____ About _____

_____

_____ About _____

_____

_____ About _____

_____

Things that frightened or concerned me today:

_____

_____

Today I am grateful for:

_____

_____

Other thoughts or experiences I want to remember:

_____

_____

_____

_____

_____

☐ Su   ☐ Mo   ☐ Tu   ☐ We   ☐ Th   ☐ Fr   ☐ Sa

Date _____

How I feel today (physically): _____

How I feel today (emotionally): _____

Medication I Took

Morning _____

_____

Afternoon _____

_____

Evening _____

_____

What I Ate

Morning _____

_____

Afternoon _____

_____

Evening _____

_____

Glasses of Water

Today I talked to:

_____ About _____

_____ About _____

_____ About _____

_____About _____

Things that frightened or concerned me today:

_____

_____

Today I am grateful for:

_____

_____

Other thoughts or experiences I want to remember:

_____

_____

_____

_____

_____

☐Su ☐Mo ☐Tu ☐We ☐Th ☐Fr ☐Sa

Date _____

How I feel today (physically): _____

How I feel today (emotionally): _____

Medication I Took

Morning _____

_____

Afternoon _____

_____

Evening _____

_____

What I Ate

Morning _____

_____

Afternoon _____

_____

Evening _____

_____

Glasses of Water

Today I talked to:

_____ About _____

_____

_____ About _____

_____

_____ About _____

_____

_____ About _____

_____

Things that frightened or concerned me today:

_____

_____

Today I am grateful for:

_____

_____

Other thoughts or experiences I want to remember:

_____

_____

_____

_____

_____

☐Su   ☐Mo   ☐Tu   ☐We   ☐Th   ☐Fr   ☐Sa

Date _____

How I feel today (physically): _____

How I feel today (emotionally): _____

Medication I Took

Morning _____

_____

Afternoon _____

_____

Evening _____

_____

What I Ate

Morning _____

_____

Afternoon _____

_____

Evening _____

_____

Glasses of Water

Today I talked to:

_____ About _____

_____ About _____

_____ About _____

_____ About _____

Things that frightened or concerned me today:

_____

_____

Today I am grateful for:

_____

_____

Other thoughts or experiences I want to remember:

_____

_____

_____

_____

_____

☐Su ☐Mo ☐Tu ☐We ☐Th ☐Fr ☐Sa

Date _____

How I feel today (physically): _____

How I feel today (emotionally): _____

Medication I Took

Morning _____

_____

Afternoon _____

_____

Evening _____

_____

What I Ate

Morning _____

_____

Afternoon _____

_____

Evening _____

_____

Glasses of Water

Today I talked to:

_____ About _____

_____

_____ About _____

_____

_____ About _____

_____

_____About _____

_____

Things that frightened or concerned me today:

_____

_____

Today I am grateful for:

_____

_____

Other thoughts or experiences I want to remember:

_____

_____

_____

_____

_____

☐Su   ☐Mo   ☐Tu   ☐We   ☐Th   ☐Fr   ☐Sa

Date _____

How I feel today (physically): _____

How I feel today (emotionally): _____

Medication I Took

Morning _____

_____

Afternoon _____

_____

Evening _____

_____

What I Ate

Morning _____

_____

Afternoon _____

_____

Evening _____

_____

Glasses of Water

Today I talked to:

_____ About _____

_____

_____ About _____

_____

_____ About _____

_____

_____ About _____

_____

Things that frightened or concerned me today:

_____

_____

Today I am grateful for:

_____

_____

Other thoughts or experiences I want to remember:

_____

_____

_____

_____

_____

☐ Su   ☐ Mo   ☐ Tu   ☐ We   ☐ Th   ☐ Fr   ☐ Sa

Date _____

How I feel today (physically): _____

How I feel today (emotionally): _____

Medication I Took

Morning _____

_____

Afternoon _____

_____

Evening _____

_____

What I Ate

Morning _____

_____

Afternoon _____

_____

Evening _____

_____

Glasses of Water

Today I talked to:

_____ About _____

_____

_____ About _____

_____

_____ About _____

_____

_____ About _____

_____

Things that frightened or concerned me today:

_____

_____

Today I am grateful for:

_____

_____

Other thoughts or experiences I want to remember:

_____

_____

_____

_____

_____

☐ Su   ☐ Mo   ☐ Tu   ☐ We   ☐ Th   ☐ Fr   ☐ Sa

Date _____

How I feel today (physically): _____

How I feel today (emotionally): _____

Medication I Took

Morning _____

_____

Afternoon _____

_____

Evening _____

_____

What I Ate

Morning _____

_____

Afternoon _____

_____

Evening _____

_____

Glasses of Water

Today I talked to:

_____ About _____

_____ About _____

_____ About _____

_____ About _____

_____

Things that frightened or concerned me today:

_____

_____

Today I am grateful for:

_____

_____

Other thoughts or experiences I want to remember:

_____

_____

_____

_____

_____

☐ Su   ☐ Mo   ☐ Tu   ☐ We   ☐ Th   ☐ Fr   ☐ Sa

Date   _____

How I feel today (physically): _____

How I feel today (emotionally): _____

Medication I Took

Morning _____

_____

Afternoon _____

_____

Evening _____

_____

What I Ate

Morning _____

_____

Afternoon _____

_____

Evening _____

_____

Glasses of Water

Today I talked to:

_____ About _____

_____

_____ About _____

_____

_____ About _____

_____

_____ About _____

_____

Things that frightened or concerned me today:

_____

_____

Today I am grateful for:

_____

_____

Other thoughts or experiences I want to remember:

_____

_____

_____

_____

_____

☐ Su　　☐ Mo　　☐ Tu　　☐ We　　☐ Th　　☐ Fr　　☐ Sa

Date _____

How I feel today (physically): _____

How I feel today (emotionally): _____

Medication I Took

Morning _____

_____

Afternoon _____

_____

Evening _____

_____

What I Ate

Morning _____

_____

Afternoon _____

_____

Evening _____

_____

Glasses of Water

Today I talked to:

_____ About _____

_____ About _____

_____ About _____

_____About _____

Things that frightened or concerned me today:

_____

_____

Today I am grateful for:

_____

_____

Other thoughts or experiences I want to remember:

_____

_____

_____

_____

_____

☐Su ☐Mo ☐Tu ☐We ☐Th ☐Fr ☐Sa

Date _____

How I feel today (physically): _____

How I feel today (emotionally): _____

Medication I Took

Morning _____

_____

Afternoon _____

_____

Evening _____

_____

What I Ate

Morning _____

_____

Afternoon _____

_____

Evening _____

_____

Glasses of Water

Today I talked to:

_____ About _____

_____

_____ About _____

_____

_____ About _____

_____

_____ About _____

_____

Things that frightened or concerned me today:

_____

_____

Today I am grateful for:

_____

_____

Other thoughts or experiences I want to remember:

_____

_____

_____

_____

_____

☐ Su   ☐ Mo   ☐ Tu   ☐ We   ☐ Th   ☐ Fr   ☐ Sa

Date _____

How I feel today (physically): _____

How I feel today (emotionally): _____

Medication I Took

Morning _____

_____

Afternoon _____

_____

Evening _____

_____

What I Ate

Morning _____

_____

Afternoon _____

_____

Evening _____

_____

Glasses of Water

Today I talked to:

_____ About _____

_____

_____ About _____

_____

_____ About _____

_____

_____ About _____

_____

Things that frightened or concerned me today:

_____

_____

Today I am grateful for:

_____

_____

Other thoughts or experiences I want to remember:

_____

_____

_____

_____

☐Su   ☐Mo   ☐Tu   ☐We   ☐Th   ☐Fr   ☐Sa

Date _____

How I feel today (physically): _____

How I feel today (emotionally): _____

Medication I Took

Morning _____

_____

Afternoon _____

_____

Evening _____

_____

What I Ate

Morning _____

_____

Afternoon _____

_____

Evening _____

_____

Glasses of Water

Today I talked to:

_____ About _____

_____

_____ About _____

_____

_____ About _____

_____

_____ About _____

_____

Things that frightened or concerned me today:

_____

_____

Today I am grateful for:

_____

_____

Other thoughts or experiences I want to remember:

_____

_____

_____

_____

_____

☐Su ☐Mo ☐Tu ☐We ☐Th ☐Fr ☐Sa

Date _____

How I feel today (physically): _____

How I feel today (emotionally): _____

Medication I Took

Morning _____

_____

Afternoon _____

_____

Evening _____

_____

What I Ate

Morning _____

_____

Afternoon _____

_____

Evening _____

_____

Glasses of Water

Today I talked to:

_____ About _____

_____ About _____

_____ About _____

_____ About _____

_____

Things that frightened or concerned me today:

_____

_____

Today I am grateful for:

_____

_____

Other thoughts or experiences I want to remember:

_____

_____

_____

_____

_____

☐Su   ☐Mo   ☐Tu   ☐We   ☐Th   ☐Fr   ☐Sa

Date _____

How I feel today (physically): _____

How I feel today (emotionally): _____

Medication I Took

Morning _____

_____

Afternoon _____

_____

Evening _____

_____

What I Ate

Morning _____

_____

Afternoon _____

_____

Evening _____

_____

Glasses of Water

Today I talked to:

_____ About _____

_____

_____ About _____

_____

_____ About _____

_____

_____ About _____

_____

Things that frightened or concerned me today:

_____

_____

Today I am grateful for:

_____

_____

Other thoughts or experiences I want to remember:

_____

_____

_____

_____

_____

☐Su   ☐Mo   ☐Tu   ☐We   ☐Th   ☐Fr   ☐Sa

Date _____

How I feel today (physically): _____

How I feel today (emotionally): _____

Medication I Took

Morning _____

_____

Afternoon _____

_____

Evening _____

_____

What I Ate

Morning _____

_____

Afternoon _____

_____

Evening _____

_____

Glasses of Water

Today I talked to:

_____ About _____

_____

_____ About _____

_____

_____ About _____

_____

_____About _____

_____

Things that frightened or concerned me today:

_____

_____

Today I am grateful for:

_____

_____

Other thoughts or experiences I want to remember:

_____

_____

_____

_____

_____

☐Su ☐Mo ☐Tu ☐We ☐Th ☐Fr ☐Sa

Date _____

How I feel today (physically): _____

How I feel today (emotionally): _____

Medication I Took

Morning _____

_____

Afternoon _____

_____

Evening _____

_____

What I Ate

Morning _____

_____

Afternoon _____

_____

Evening _____

_____

Glasses of Water

Today I talked to:

_____ About _____

_____

_____ About _____

_____

_____ About _____

_____

_____About _____

_____

Things that frightened or concerned me today:

_____

_____

Today I am grateful for:

_____

_____

Other thoughts or experiences I want to remember:

_____

_____

_____

_____

_____

☐ Su ☐ Mo ☐ Tu ☐ We ☐ Th ☐ Fr ☐ Sa

Date _____

How I feel today (physically): _____

How I feel today (emotionally): _____

Medication I Took

Morning _____

_____

Afternoon _____

_____

Evening _____

_____

What I Ate

Morning _____

_____

Afternoon _____

_____

Evening _____

_____

Glasses of Water

Today I talked to:

_____ About _____

_____

_____ About _____

_____

_____ About _____

_____

_____About _____

_____

Things that frightened or concerned me today:

_____

_____

Today I am grateful for:

_____

_____

Other thoughts or experiences I want to remember:

_____

_____

_____

_____

_____

☐Su   ☐Mo   ☐Tu   ☐We   ☐Th   ☐Fr   ☐Sa

Date   _____

How I feel today (physically): _____

How I feel today (emotionally): _____

Medication I Took

Morning _____

_____

Afternoon _____

_____

Evening _____

_____

What I Ate

Morning _____

_____

Afternoon _____

_____

Evening _____

_____

Glasses of Water

Today I talked to:

_____ About _____

_____

_____ About _____

_____

_____ About _____

_____

_____ About _____

_____

Things that frightened or concerned me today:

_____

_____

Today I am grateful for:

_____

_____

Other thoughts or experiences I want to remember:

_____

_____

_____

_____

_____

☐Su ☐Mo ☐Tu ☐We ☐Th ☐Fr ☐Sa

Date _____

How I feel today (physically): _____

How I feel today (emotionally): _____

Medication I Took

Morning _____

_____

Afternoon _____

_____

Evening _____

_____

What I Ate

Morning _____

_____

Afternoon _____

_____

Evening _____

_____

Glasses of Water

Today I talked to:

_____ About _____

_____

_____ About _____

_____

_____ About _____

_____

_____About _____

_____

Things that frightened or concerned me today:

_____

_____

Today I am grateful for:

_____

_____

Other thoughts or experiences I want to remember:

_____

_____

_____

_____

_____

☐Su ☐Mo ☐Tu ☐We ☐Th ☐Fr ☐Sa

Date _____

How I feel today (physically): _____

How I feel today (emotionally): _____

Medication I Took

Morning _____

_____

Afternoon _____

_____

Evening _____

_____

What I Ate

Morning _____

_____

Afternoon _____

_____

Evening _____

_____

Glasses of Water

Today I talked to:

_____ About _____

_____

_____ About _____

_____

_____ About _____

_____

_____About _____

_____

Things that frightened or concerned me today:

_____

_____

Today I am grateful for:

_____

_____

Other thoughts or experiences I want to remember:

_____

_____

_____

_____

_____

☐ Su ☐ Mo ☐ Tu ☐ We ☐ Th ☐ Fr ☐ Sa

Date _____

How I feel today (physically): _____

How I feel today (emotionally): _____

Medication I Took

Morning _____

_____

Afternoon _____

_____

Evening _____

_____

What I Ate

Morning _____

_____

Afternoon _____

_____

Evening _____

_____

Glasses of Water

Today I talked to:

_____ About _____

_____

_____ About _____

_____

_____ About _____

_____

_____ About _____

_____

Things that frightened or concerned me today:

_____

_____

Today I am grateful for:

_____

_____

Other thoughts or experiences I want to remember:

_____

_____

_____

_____

_____

☐ Su   ☐ Mo   ☐ Tu   ☐ We   ☐ Th   ☐ Fr   ☐ Sa

Date _____

How I feel today (physically): _____

How I feel today (emotionally): _____

Medication I Took

Morning _____

_____

Afternoon _____

_____

Evening _____

_____

What I Ate

Morning _____

_____

Afternoon _____

_____

Evening _____

_____

Glasses of Water

Today I talked to:

_____ About _____

_____

_____ About _____

_____

_____ About _____

_____

_____ About _____

_____

Things that frightened or concerned me today:

_____

_____

Today I am grateful for:

_____

_____

Other thoughts or experiences I want to remember:

_____

_____

_____

_____

_____

☐ Su   ☐ Mo   ☐ Tu   ☐ We   ☐ Th   ☐ Fr   ☐ Sa

Date _____

How I feel today (physically): _____

How I feel today (emotionally): _____

Medication I Took

Morning _____

_____

Afternoon _____

_____

Evening _____

_____

What I Ate

Morning _____

_____

Afternoon _____

_____

Evening _____

_____

Glasses of Water

Today I talked to:

_____ About _____

_____
_____ About _____

_____
_____ About _____

_____
_____About _____

_____

Things that frightened or concerned me today:

_____
_____

Today I am grateful for:

_____
_____

Other thoughts or experiences I want to remember:

_____
_____
_____
_____
_____

☐ Su   ☐ Mo   ☐ Tu   ☐ We   ☐ Th   ☐ Fr   ☐ Sa

Date _____

How I feel today (physically): _____

How I feel today (emotionally): _____

Medication I Took

Morning _____

_____

Afternoon _____

_____

Evening _____

_____

What I Ate

Morning _____

_____

Afternoon _____

_____

Evening _____

_____

Glasses of Water

Today I talked to:

_____ About _____

_____

_____ About _____

_____

_____ About _____

_____

_____About _____

_____

Things that frightened or concerned me today:

_____

_____

Today I am grateful for:

_____

_____

Other thoughts or experiences I want to remember:

_____

_____

_____

_____

_____

☐Su ☐Mo ☐Tu ☐We ☐Th ☐Fr ☐Sa

Date _____

How I feel today (physically): _____

How I feel today (emotionally): _____

Medication I Took

Morning _____

_____

Afternoon _____

_____

Evening _____

_____

What I Ate

Morning _____

_____

Afternoon _____

_____

Evening _____

_____

Glasses of Water

Today I talked to:

_____ About _____

_____

_____ About _____

_____

_____ About _____

_____

_____ About _____

_____

Things that frightened or concerned me today:

_____

_____

Today I am grateful for:

_____

_____

Other thoughts or experiences I want to remember:

_____

_____

_____

_____

_____

☐ Su   ☐ Mo   ☐ Tu   ☐ We   ☐ Th   ☐ Fr   ☐ Sa

Date _____

How I feel today (physically): _____

How I feel today (emotionally): _____

Medication I Took

Morning _____

_____

Afternoon _____

_____

Evening _____

_____

What I Ate

Morning _____

_____

Afternoon _____

_____

Evening _____

_____

Glasses of Water

Today I talked to:

_____ About _____

_____

_____ About _____

_____

_____ About _____

_____

_____ About _____

_____

Things that frightened or concerned me today:

_____

_____

Today I am grateful for:

_____

_____

Other thoughts or experiences I want to remember:

_____

_____

_____

_____

_____

☐Su   ☐Mo   ☐Tu   ☐We   ☐Th   ☐Fr   ☐Sa

Date   _____

How I feel today (physically): _____

How I feel today (emotionally): _____

Medication I Took

Morning _____

_____

Afternoon _____

_____

Evening   _____

_____

What I Ate

Morning _____

_____

Afternoon _____

_____

Evening _____

_____

Glasses of Water

☐   ☐   ☐   ☐

☐   ☐   ☐   ☐

Today I talked to:

_____ About _____

_____ About _____

_____ About _____

_____About _____

Things that frightened or concerned me today:

_____

_____

Today I am grateful for:

_____

_____

Other thoughts or experiences I want to remember:

_____

_____

_____

_____

_____

☐Su   ☐Mo   ☐Tu   ☐We   ☐Th   ☐Fr   ☐Sa

Date _____

How I feel today (physically): _____

How I feel today (emotionally): _____

Medication I Took

Morning _____

_____

Afternoon _____

_____

Evening _____

_____

What I Ate

Morning _____

_____

Afternoon _____

_____

Evening _____

_____

Glasses of Water

Today I talked to:

_____ About _____

_____

_____ About _____

_____

_____ About _____

_____

_____ About _____

_____

Things that frightened or concerned me today:

_____

_____

Today I am grateful for:

_____

_____

Other thoughts or experiences I want to remember:

_____

_____

_____

_____

_____

☐Su   ☐Mo   ☐Tu   ☐We   ☐Th   ☐Fr   ☐Sa

Date _____

How I feel today (physically): _____

How I feel today (emotionally): _____

Medication I Took

Morning _____

_____

Afternoon _____

_____

Evening _____

_____

What I Ate

Morning _____

_____

Afternoon _____

_____

Evening _____

_____

Glasses of Water

Today I talked to:

_____ About _____

_____

_____ About _____

_____

_____ About _____

_____

_____About _____

_____

Things that frightened or concerned me today:

_____

_____

Today I am grateful for:

_____

_____

Other thoughts or experiences I want to remember:

_____

_____

_____

_____

_____

Thanks so much for purchasing this journal!

To see our full collection of journals, please visit
ProfessionalContentCreation.com/Journals

Made in United States
Troutdale, OR
10/05/2023

13429789R00083